Tammy's
Original/Gluten Free Cookbook

TAMMY AIKEN

ISBN 978-1-953223-08-1 (paperback)

Copyright © 2020 by Tammy Aiken

All rights reserved. No part of this publication may be reproduced, distributed, or transmitted in any form or by any means, including photocopying, recording, or other electronic or mechanical methods without the prior written permission of the publisher. For permission requests, solicit the publisher via the address below.

Rushmore Press LLC
1 800 460 9188
www.rushmorepress.com

Printed in the United States of America

Contents

Introduction 5

Original Black Moist Brownies 7

Gluten Free and Dairy Free Moist Black Brownies 8

Original Peanut Butter and Jelly Cookies 9

Gluten Free and Dairy Free Peanut Butter Jelly Cookies 10

Original Cake Brownies 11

Gluten Free and Dairy Free Cake Brownies 12

Original Chai Cookies 13

Gluten Free and Dairy Free Chai Cookies 14

Original Christmas Thumb Print Cookies 15

Gluten Free Christmas Thumb Print Cookies 16

Original Lemon Bars 17

Gluten Free Lemon Bars 18

Original Lemon Cookies 19

Gluten Free and Dairy Free Lemon Cookies 20

Original No Bake Peanut Butter Pie 21

Gluten Free and Dairy Free Peanut Butter Cookies For No Bake Peanut Butter Pie 22

Gluten Free and Dairy Free Peanut Butter Cookie Crust 23

Gluten Free or Gluten Free Dairy Free No Bake Peanut Butter Pie 24

Original Dried Cranberry Oatmeal White Morsel Cookies 25

Gluten Free and Dairy Free Dried Cranberry White Morsels Cookies 26

Original Peanut Butter Cookies 27

Gluten Free and Dairy Free Peanut Butter Cookies 28

Original Pumpkin Bread 29

Gluten Free and and Dairy Free Pumpkin Bread 30

Buttercream Cream Cheese Gluten Free Frosting 31

Original Butternut Squash Bars with Cream Cheese Frosting 32

Gluten Free and Dairy Free Butternut Squash Bars 33

Gluten Free Cream Cheese Frosting 34

Original Peppermint Santa's 35

Dairy Free Gluten Free Peppermint Santa's 36

Original Zucchini Bread 37

Gluten Free and Dairy Free Zucchini Bread 38

Gluten Free & Dairy Free Blueberry Muffins 39

Original Blueberry Muffins 40

Ingredient Information 41

Introduction

Hi there! It is really great to share my recipes with all of you. I have created this cookbook to help people who have Celiac disease my sister-n-law has this disease I see how she suffers but she loves her sweets so I started to create gluten free recipes. You don't have to spend a lot of money on the ingredients for my gluten free recipes. It's not like you have to buy three to four different flours just to make one baked good. I used King Arthur Gluten free measure to measure flour and King Arthur Gluten free multipurpose flour.

I want people who have this disease to enjoy desserts. It really stinks when you see someone with a baked good but you can't have it. Not fair! You can eat the same desserts as your family and not feel left out. When creating this cookbook I had a lot of taste testers and people with Celiac disease so I know these recipes are a go! But of course you know the texture of the gluten free is different. The taste testers that tasted my gluten free baked goods said they had stopped buying the gluten free baked goods in the stores because of the gritty texture. Now they are enjoying my sweets.

Original Black Moist Brownies

- 2 eggs
- ½ cup granulated sugar
- ½ cup light brown sugar
- 3 tablespoons King Arthur black cocoa or Hershey's cocoa special dark
- 1 teaspoon baking soda
- ½ teaspoon baking powder
- 1/3 cup cool water
- 1 tablespoon canola oil
- 1 cup all purpose flour
- ½ to ¾ cups original Mini chocolate chips
- 7" x 11" baking pan

Preheat oven to 350 degrees. In a mixing bowl add first eight ingredients mix scraping the bowl add the flour all at once mix. Add the chocolate chips mix in with a spoon spray a baking pan with a nonstick cooking spray lightly pour batter into a baking a pan spread evenly bake for 25 minutes transfer to a cooling rack.

Note: I used King Arthur black cocoa for these brownies. If you want these brownies a little chewy add ¾ cups of chocolate chips.

Gluten Free and Dairy Free Moist Black Brownies

- 2 eggs
- ½ cup granulated sugar
- ½ cup light brown sugar
- 3 tablespoons King Arthur's black cocoa or Hershey's cocoa special dark
- 1 teaspoon Clabber Girl baking soda or Arm Hammer baking soda
- ½ teaspoon Rumford baking powder
- 1/3 cup cool water
- 1 tablespoon canola oil
- 1 cup King Arthur Gluten free Measure For Measure Flour
- ½ to ¾ cups Enjoy Life semi-sweet mini chips
- 7" x 11" baking pan

Preheat oven to 350 degrees. In a mixing bowl add the first eight ingredients mix scraping the bowl add the flour all at once mix. Add the mini chocolate chips mix in with a spoon spray the baking pan with Pam nonstick cooking spray lightly (original only) pour batter into the baking pan spread evenly bake for 25 minutes transfer to a cooling rack.

> Note: I used King Arthur black cocoa for these brownies. If you want the brownies a little chewy add ¾ cups semisweet chocolate chips

Original Peanut Butter and Jelly Cookies

- 1 cup white bread crumbs, 6 slices of fresh white bread
- 2 eggs
- 1 cup smooth peanut butter
- ½ stick softened unsalted butter
- ½ cup light brown sugar
- 1 cup granulated sugar
- 1 teaspoon baking soda
- ½ teaspoon baking powder
- 2 cups all purpose flour
- Welch's grape jelly

Preheat oven to 350 degrees. Add six bread slices to a food processor to make bread crumbs. Add breads crumbs to the mixing bowl adding the next seven ingredients. Mix scraping the bowl. Add the flour half cup at a time mix, spray a cookie sheet with a nonstick cooking spray. Make the dough balls as big as a walnut shell place in the palm of your hand and flatten out not to thin place on the cookie sheet add one teaspoon of grape jelly in the middle of each cookie and make the tops of the cookies the same way you made the bottoms place on top crimp the edges with a fork. Bake for 20 to 25 minutes transfer to a cooliing rack.

> Note: Use only slices of white bread (not the the already made bread crumbs). If you have bread crumbs left over put into a freezer bag label use for another time. Thaw the bread crumbs before using.

Gluten Free and Dairy Free Peanut Butter Jelly Cookies

- 1 ½ cups gluten free white bread crumbs, 6 slices of gluten free bread
- 2 eggs
- 1 cup Smucker's gluten free smooth peanut butter
- 2 tablespoons softened Earth Balance Vegan butter
- ½ cup light brown sugar
- 1 cup granulated sugar
- 1 teaspoon Clabber Girl baking soda or Arm and Hammer baking soda
- ½ teaspoon Rumford baking powder
- 2 cups King Arthur Gluten free Measure For Measure Flour
- Welch's concord grape jelly

Preheat oven to 300 degrees. Add the six bread slices to a food processor to make bread crumbs. Add bread crumbs to the mixing bowl adding the next seven ingredients. Mix scraping the bowl. Add the flour half a cup at a time until gone. Roll the dough balls a big as a walnut shell place in the palm of your hand and flatten out not to thin. Spray a cookie sheet with **Pam** nonstick cooking spray (original only). Place a teaspoon of the grape jelly in the middle. Make your top to your cookie just like you did with the bottoms and place on top crimp the edges with a fork. Bake for 20 to 25 minutes transfer to a cooling rack.

Note: The mixture may look a little crumbly but it will come together. If you have bread crumbs left over put into a freezer bag and label the bag use them for another time. Thaw out the bread crumbs first before using.

Original Cake Brownies

- 2 eggs
- 1 cup granulated sugar
- 1 teaspoon baking soda
- ½ teaspoon baking powder
- 3 tablespoons King Arthur black cocoa or Hershey's cocoa special dark unsweetened
- 1/3 cup cool water
- 1 cup all purpose flour
- 1/3 cup mini chocolate chips
- 7" x 11" baking pan

Preheat oven to 350 degrees. In a mixing bowl add the first six ingredients mix scraping the bowl add the flour all at once and mix. Add the chocolate chips and mix with a spoon. Spray the baking pan with nonstick cooking spray pour batter into baking pan spread out evenly bake for 25 minutes transfer to a cooling rack.

Gluten Free and Dairy Free Cake Brownies

- 2 eggs
- 1 cup granulated sugar
- 1 teaspoon Clabber Girl baking soda or Arm and Hammer baking soda
- ½ teaspoon Rumford baking powder
- 3 tablespoons King Arthur's black cocoa or Hershey's cocoa special dark unsweetened
- 1/3 cup cool water
- 1 cup King Arthur Gluten free Measure For Measure Flour
- 1/3 cup Enjoy Life semi-sweet chocolate mini chips
- 7" x 11" baking pan

Preheat oven to 350 degrees. In a mixing bowl add the first six ingredients mix scraping the bowl add the flour all at once and mix. Add the chocolate chips mix in with a spoon. Spray the baking pan with Pam nonstick cooking spray (original only) pour batter into baking pan spread out evenly bake for 25 minutes transfer to a cooling rack.

Original Chai Cookies

- 2 eggs
- 1 teaspoon baking soda
- 1 cup granulated sugar
- ½ cup light brown sugar
- ½ stick softened unsalted butter
- 1 1/8 teaspoon King Arthur chai spice
- 2 cups all purpose flour

Preheat oven to 300 degrees. In a mixing bowl add first six ingredients and mix scraping the bowl add the flour one cup at a time. Spray the cookie sheet with a nonstick cooking spray roll dough into a ball as big as a walnut shell place on a cookie sheet press on the top of the cookie lightly to flatten bake for 20 to 25 minutes transfer to a cooling rack.

Gluten Free and Dairy Free Chai Cookies

- 2 eggs
- 1 teaspoon Clabber Girl baking soda or Arm and Hammer baking soda
- 1 cup granulated sugar
- ½ cup light brown sugar
- 4 ½ tablespoons softened Earth Balance Vegan butter stick
- 1 teaspoon and 1/8 teaspoon King Arthur chai spice
- 1 ½ cups King Arthur Gluten free Measure For Measure Flour

Preheat oven to 300 degrees. In a mixing bowl add first six ingredients and mix scraping the bowl. Add the flour half cup at a time spray a cookie sheet with a Pam nonstick cooking spray (original only). Roll dough into a ball as big as a walnut shell place on a cookie sheet and press on the top of the cookie lightly to flatten bake for 20 to 25 minutes transfer to a cooling rack.

Original Christmas Thumb Print Cookies

- 2 eggs
- 1 ½ softened sticks unsalted butter
- 1 cup granulated sugar
- ¾ cup light brown sugar
- 1 teaspoon vanilla extract
- 3 ounces softened cream cheese
- 2 teaspoons baking soda
- 4 ½ cups all purpose flour
- 2 ¾ cups white morsels, reserve 2 cups
- ½ Jar Polaner strawberry jam

Preheat oven to 350 degrees. Add to a mixing bowl the first seven ingredients and mix. Add the flour half cup at a time until combined. Add the white morsels and mix in with a spoon. Take a cookie sheet and spray with a nonstick cooking spray. Roll cookie dough as big as a walnut shell. Make a thumb print in each cookie add 1 teaspoon of the strawberry jam. Bake for 25 to 30 minutes transfer to a cooling rack. Add 2 cups white chocolate chips to a glass microwave bowl melt for 30 seconds at a time mixing until smooth. Take a fork and drizzle over cookies while still warm.

Gluten Free Christmas Thumb Print Cookies

- 2 eggs
- 1 ½ sticks Earth Balance Vegan butter
- 1 cup granulated sugar
- ¾ cup light brown sugar
- 2 teaspoons pure vanilla extract
- 2 teaspoons Clabber Girl baking soda or Arm and Hammer baking soda
- 3 ounces softened Philadelphia cream cheese
- 4 cups King Arthur Gluten free Measure For Measure Flour
- 2 ¾ cups Pascha Organic white baking chips, reserve 2 cups
- ½ jar of Polaner strawberry jam

Preheat oven to 300 degrees. In a mixing bowl add the first seven ingredients and mix scraping the bowl a few times. Add the flour one cup at a time until combined. Roll the cookie dough as big as a walnut shell spray a cookie sheet with **Pam** nonstick cooking spray (original only). Make a thumb print in the middle of each cookie fill with one teaspoon of jam. Bake for 25 to 30 minutes transfer to a cooling rack to cool. Add 2 cups white chocolate chips to a glass microwave bowl melt for 30 seconds at a time mixing until smooth. Melt for 30 seconds at a time mixing until smooth. Drizzle over warm cookies.

Original Lemon Bars

- 2 eggs
- 1 teaspoon baking soda
- 1/8 teaspoon baking powder
- 1 stick softened unsalted butter
- 1 cup granulated sugar
- 2 tablespoons canola oil
- 3 ounces softened cream cheese
- 3.4 ounce box Jello instant lemon pudding pie filling
- ½ teaspoon sea salt
- 1 tablespoon fresh lemon zest
- ¼ cup fresh lemon juice
- 2 ½ cups all purpose flour

Preheat oven to 350 degrees. In a mixing bowl add the first eleven ingredients and mix. Add the flour half a cup at a time mix scraping the bowl.

Spray a 9"x 13" baking pan with a nonstick cooking pour batter into baking pan spread evenly bake for 20 to 25 minutes transfer to cooling rack.

Lemon Glaze

- 1 cup confectionery sugar
- ½ tablespoon lemon zest
- 2 tablespoons and ½ teaspoon lemon

In a bowl add all three ingredients and whisk until smooth pour over the hot lemons bars spread and let cool.

Gluten Free Lemon Bars

- 2 eggs
- 1 cup granulated sugar
- 1 tablespoon fresh lemon zest
- ¼ cup fresh lemon juice
- 1 stick softened Earth Balance Vegan butter stick
- ½ teaspoon sea salt
- 1 teaspoon Clabber Girl baking soda or Arm and Hammer baking soda
- ⅛ teaspoon Rumford baking powder
- 2 tablespoons canola oil
- 3 ounces softened Philadelphia cream cheese
- 2 ½ cups King Arthur Gluten free Measure For Measure Flour

Preheat oven to 350 degrees. In a mixing bowl add the first nine ingredients mix on high for 30 seconds. Add cream cheese start slow going to high speed for 30 seconds. Add the flour half cup at a time until gone spray a 9"x 13" baking pan with a Pam nonstick cooking spray (original only). Pour batter into baking pan spread the batter evenly bake for 20 to 25 minutes transfer to a cooling rack.

Lemon Glaze

- 1 cup confectionery sugar
- ½ tablespoon lemon zest
- 2 tablespoons and ½ teaspoon lemon juice
- In a small bowl add the three ingredients and whisk until smooth. Pour and spread over warm lemon bars, let cool.

Original Lemon Cookies

- 2 eggs
- 1 cup granulated sugar
- 1 teaspoon baking soda
- zest of 1 lemon
- 2 ½ tablespoons softened unsalted butter
- 2 cups all purpose flour

Preheat oven to 350 degrees. In a mixing bowl add the first six ingredients and mix. Add flour half a cup at a time scraping the bowl. Spray a cookie sheet with a nonstick cooking spray. Drop cookie dough by teaspoonfuls onto a cookie sheet. Bake for 20 to 22 minutes transfer to a cooling rack.

Lemon Glaze

- 1 cup confectionery sugar
- 1 teaspoon lemon zest
- juice of a ½ lemon

In a bowl add all the ingredients and whisk until smooth. Dip warm cookies into the glaze or drizzle over cookies with a fork let the glaze set up.

Gluten Free and Dairy Free Lemon Cookies

- 2 eggs
- 1 cup granulated sugar
- 3 tablespoons softened Earth Balance Vegan butter sticks
- 1 teaspoon Clabber Girl baking soda or Arm and Hammer baking soda
- zest of 1 lemon
- 1 tablespoon 100% lemon juice
- 2 cups King Arthur Gluten free Measure For Measure Flour

Preheat oven to 300 degrees. In a mixing bowl add first six ingredients and mix. Add the flour one cup at a time mix well spray a cookie sheet with **Pam** nonstick cooking spray (original only). Bake for 20 to 22 minutes transfer to a cooling rack.

Lemon Glaze

- 1 cup confectionery sugar
- 1 teaspoon fresh lemon zest
- juice of a ½ lemon

In a mixing bowl add all three ingredients and whisk. Dip the top of the cookies into the glaze or drizzle over cookies with a fork let the glaze set up.

Original No Bake Peanut Butter Pie

Crust

- 15 whole Nutter Butter Peanut butter cookies, reserve ¼ to a ½ cup
- 2 tablespoons melted unsalted butter

Add the cookies to a food processor and process like sand. Add the melted butter to the cookie crumbs pulse until incorporated. Add to a 9 inch glass pie dish pat the crust on the bottom and half way up the sides put in the refrigerator while you make the filling.

Filling

- 1 cup smooth peanut butter
- 7 ounces softened cream cheese
- 1 ½ cups confectionery sugar
- 3 tablespoons 1% milk
- 2 cups cool whip, reserve 1 cup

In a mixing bowl add first four ingredients start to mix on low when the mixture starts to come together then whip on high for 30 seconds. Add the one cup of cool whip to the mixture and mix in with a spoon add the filling to the pie crust spread evenly. Take the reserved 1 cup of cool whip and spread over the top take the reserved cookies sprinkle over the top put pie into the refrigerator for 1 hour.

Gluten Free and Dairy Free Peanut Butter Cookies For No Bake Peanut Butter Pie

- 2 eggs
- 1 cup gluten free smooth peanut butter
- 1 teaspoon Clabber Girl baking soda
- 1 cup granulated sugar
- ½ cup light brown sugar
- 3 tablespoons softened Earth Balance Vegan butter stick
- ⅛ teaspoon sea salt
- 1 cup king Arthur Gluten free Measure For Measure Flour

Preheat oven to 300 degrees. In a mixing bowl add the first seven ingredients and mix add the flour all at once mix until incorporated spray a cookie sheet with **Pam** nonstick cooking spray (original only). Roll cookie dough as big as a walnut shell place on the cookie sheet take a fork and press lightly on top of the cookie to flatten a little. Bake for 20 minutes transfer to a cooling rack.

Gluten Free and Dairy Free Peanut Butter Cookie Crust

In a food processor add 6 ½ gluten free peanut butter cookies process until like sand. Add 3 tablespoons of melted Earth Balance Vegan butter to the cookie crumbs and mix reserving a ¼ cup of the cookie crumbs you can reserve more cookie crumbs it's all up to you. Add to a 9" pie dish pat crumbs on the bottom and half way up the sides put in the refrigerator while you make the filling.

Gluten Free or Gluten Free Dairy Free No Bake Peanut Butter Pie

- 1 cup any gluten free smooth peanut butter
- 3 tablespoons water or Lactose milk
- 1 ½ cups confectionery sugar
- 7 ounces softened Philadelphia cream cheese or substitute with 8 ounces Tofutti cream cheese (plain) milk free for milk allergies
- 2 cups cool whip reserve 1 cup or people with milk allergies can substitute cool whip for Truwhip or Coco Whip Dairy free

In a mixing bowl mix the first three ingredients starting off slow to mix then whip for a few minutes until all combine scraping the bowl. Add the one cup of cool whip mix with a spoon until all incorporated in the mixture. Take the pie crust out of the refrigerator and fill the crust with the filling spread evenly then take the reserved cool whip spread over the top. Sprinkle with the ¼ of cup cookie crumbs that you reserved put the pie back into the refrigerator for 1 hour to set up.

Original Dried Cranberry Oatmeal White Morsel Cookies

- 2 eggs
- 4 tablespoons softened unsalted butter
- 1 cup granulated sugar
- ½ cup light brown sugar
- ¼ teaspoon sea salt
- 1 teaspoon baking soda
- 1 teaspoon pure vanilla extract
- 1 ½ cups quick cooking oats
- 1 ½ cups all purpose flour
- ¾ cup dried cranberries
- ¾ cups white morsels

Preheat oven to 350 degrees. In a mixing bowl add first seven ingredients and mix scraping the bowl. Add the oatmeal and flour mix add the last two ingredients and mix with a spoon. Spray a cookie sheet with a nonstick cooking spray roll the cookie dough as big as a walnut shell and press down on the top of the cookies gently make sure you have space between each cookie bake for 20 to 25 minutes transfer to a cooling rack.

Gluten Free and Dairy Free Dried Cranberry White Morsels Cookies

- 1 ½ cups Quaker Oats gluten free quick cooking oatmeal
- 2 eggs
- 6 tablespoons softened Earth Balance Vegan butter sticks, reserve 2 tablespoons
- ½ cup light brown sugar
- 1 cup granulated sugar
- 1 teaspoon Clabber Girl baking soda or Arm and Hammer baking soda
- ¼ teaspoon sea salt
- 1 ½ teaspoons pure vanilla extract
- 2 cups King Arthur Gluten free Measure For Measure Flour
- ¾ cup Ocean Spray dried cranberries
- ¾ cup Pascha Organic White baking chips

Preheat oven to 300 degrees. In a frying pan add the two tablespoons of butter let melt add the all the oatmeal cook for one minute on medium low heat mix watch this so it does not burn. Transfer to a bowl let cool some, in a mixing bowl add next seven ingredients and mix add the flour one cup at a time mix until combined. Add the cooked oatmeal and cranberries mix in with a spoon, scraping the bowl. Add the Pascha Organic white baking chips mix in with a spoon. Spray a cookie sheet with Pam nonstick cooking spray (original only). Roll the dough as big as a walnut shell press down the top of the cookies gently bake for 25 to 30 minutes transfer to a cooling rack.

Original Peanut Butter Cookies

- 2 eggs
- 1 cup smooth peanut butter
- 1 teaspoon baking soda
- 1 cup granulated sugar
- ½ cup light brown sugar
- 4 tablespoons softened unsalted butter
- ⅛ teaspoon sea salt
- 1 cup all purpose flour

Preheat oven to 350 degrees. In a mixing bowl add the first seven ingredients mix scraping the bowl add the flour all at once mix spray a cookie sheet with a nonstick cooking spray lightly. Roll cookie dough as big as a walnut shell place on cookie sheet take a fork press down on top of the cookie lightly until you see fork marks bake for 20 minutes transfer to a cooling rack.

Gluten Free and Dairy Free Peanut Butter Cookies

- 2 eggs
- 1 cup gluten free smooth peanut butter
- 1 teaspoon Clabber Girl baking soda or Arm and Hammer baking soda
- 1 cup granulated sugar
- ½ cup light brown sugar
- 3 tablespoons softened Earth Balance Vegan butter
- ⅛ teaspoon sea salt
- 1 cup king Arthur Gluten free Measure For Measure Flour

Preheat oven to 300 degrees. In a mixing bowl add the first seven ingredients and mix add the flour all at once mix scraping the bowl. Spray a cookie sheet with Pam nonstick cooking spray lightly (original only). Roll cookie dough as big as a walnut shell place on the cookie sheet take a fork and press lightly on the cookie until you see fork marks. Bake for 20 minutes transfer to a cooling rack.

Original Pumpkin Bread

- 2 eggs
- 1 cup granulated sugar
- ¼ teaspoon sea salt
- 1 teaspoon King Arthur Vietnamese Cinnamon or original ground cinnamon
- ⅛ teaspoon ground clove
- ¼ teaspoon ground ginger
- ½ teaspoon fresh nutmeg or original ground nutmeg
- ½ teaspoon baking soda
- 1 teaspoon baking powder
- 1 cup 100% canned pumpkin
- 1 cup all purpose flour
- ½ cup chopped walnuts, optional

Preheat the oven to 300 degrees for the first 10 minutes then turn heat at up to 350 degrees. In a mixing bowl add the first ten ingredients mix scraping the bowl add the flour and mix. Spray a glass loaf baking pan with a nonstick cooking spray lightly. Pour batter into loaf pan spread evenly bake for 65 to 66 minutes transfer to a cooling rack.

Buttercream Cream Cheese Frosting

- 4 ounces softened cream cheese
- 1 tablespoon softened unsalted butter
- ½ cup confectioner sugar
- 1 tablespoon 1% milk
- King Arthur pumpkin sugar, optional

In a mixing bowl add the first two ingredients mix. On high mix for 20 seconds scraping the bowl. Add the next two ingredients mix on high for 20 seconds scraping the bowl. Spread on cool bread.

Gluten Free and and Dairy Free Pumpkin Bread

- 2 eggs
- 1 cup granulated sugar
- ¼ teaspoon sea salt
- 1 teaspoon King Arthur Vietnamese cinnamon
- ⅛ teaspoon King Arthur ground clove
- ¼ teaspoon King Arthur ground ginger
- ½ teaspoon fresh nutmeg or King Arthur ground nutmeg
- ½ teaspoon Clabber girl baking soda or Arm and Hammer baking soda
- 1 teaspoon Rumford baking powder
- 1 cup Libby's 100% canned pumpkin
- 1 cup King Arthur Gluten free Measure For Measure Flour
- ½ cup chopped walnuts, optional

Preheat oven to 300 degrees for the first ten minutes then turn the oven to 350 degrees. In a mixing bowl add first ten ingredients and mix scraping the bowl then add the flour mix. Spray a glass loaf baking dish with Pam nonstick cooking spray (original only). Pour batter into the loaf pan and spread evenly put into the oven bake for 65 to 66 minutes transfer to a cooking rack.

Buttercream Cream Cheese Gluten Free Frosting

- 4 ounces softened Philadelphia cream cheese
- 1 tablespoon softened Earth Balance Vegan butter stick
- ½ cup confectionery sugar
- 1 tablespoon Lactose 1% milk or cool water, not cold
- King Arthur pumpkin sugar, optional

In a mixing bowl add the first two ingredients mix on high for 20 seconds. Add next two ingredients mix on high 20 seconds more. Spread on cool bread.

Buttercream Cream Cheese Gluten Free Dairy Free Frosting

- 1 stick Earth Balance Vegan butter stick
- 8 ounce Tofutti cream cheese plain-dairy free
- 4 ½ cups confectionery sugar
- ¼ teaspoon sea salt
- 2 tablespoons pure vanilla extract
- King Arthur pumpkin sugar, optional

In a mixing bowl add the first two ingredients mix. Add the next three ingredients mix well. Put in the refrigerator for at least one hour to set up a little before you spread on the cooled bread just use half of this it makes a lot then spread on cooled pumpkin bread just keep in mind the texture will be different.

Original Butternut Squash Bars with Cream Cheese Frosting

- 2 eggs
- 1/3 cup canola oil
- 1 tablespoon Grandma's Molasses
- 1/8 teaspoon sea salt
- ½ teaspoon King Arthur Vietnamese cinnamon or ground cinnamon
- pinch fresh nutmeg or King Arthur ground nutmeg or ground nutmeg
- 1 cup granulated sugar
- ½ teaspoon baking soda
- 2 teaspoons baking powder
- 1 ½ cups fresh butternut squash, peeled, cut into chunks, cooked, mashed and cooled
- 2 cups all purpose flour

Note: You will have to drain the squash for a couple of hours or overnight there will extra liquid.

Preheat oven to 350 degrees. In a mixing bowl add the first nine ingredients mix scraping the bowl. Add the squash mix add the flour half cup at a time mix well. Spray a baking pan lightly with a nonstick cooking spray pour batter into baking pan spread the batter evenly bake for 20 minutes. Transfer to a cooling rack let cool completely

Cream Cheese Frosting

- 8 ounce softened cream cheese
- 4 tablespoons softened unsalted butter
- 2 ½ cups confectionery sugar
- 1 tablespoon 1% milk

In a mixing bowl add the first two ingredients mix together scrape the bowl add the next two ingredients and mix. This may look like it won't come together but it will.

Gluten Free and Dairy Free Butternut Squash Bars

- 2 eggs
- 1/3 cup canola oil
- 1 tablespoon Grandmas Molasses
- 1/8 teaspoon sea salt
- 1 ¼ teaspoon King Arthur Vietnamese ground cinnamon or original ground cinnamon
- King Arthur's ground nutmeg or original ground nutmeg
- 1 cup granulated sugar
- ½ teaspoon Clabber Girl baking soda or Arm and Hammer baking soda
- 2 teaspoons Rumford baking powder
- 1 ½ cups fresh butternut squash peeled, cut up into chunks, cooked, mashed and cooled
- 2 cups King Arthur Gluten free Measure For Measure Flour

Note: You will have to drain the squash for a couple of hours or overnight there will be extra liquid. Read labels on your spices.

Preheat oven to 350 degrees. In a mixing bowl add first nine ingredients mix then add the cooled squash mix until combined scraping the bowl. Add the flour ½ cup at a time and mix. Spray the baking pan with Pam nonstick cooking spray cooking spray (original only). Pour batter into baking pan spread out evenly bake for 20 minutes transfer to a cooling rack.

Gluten Free Cream Cheese Frosting

- 8 ounce softened Philadelphia cream cheese
- 4 tablespoons softened Earth Balance Vegan butter stick
- 2 ½ cups confectionery sugar
- 1 tablespoon Lactose 1% milk or cool water
- In a mixing bowl add the first two ingredients mix well scraping the bowl then add the last two ingredients and mix. It may look like this won't come together but it will.

Gluten Free Dairy Free Cream Cheese Frosting

- 8 ounce Tofutti Cream Cheese plain-dairy free
- 4 ½ cups confectionery sugar
- ¼ teaspoon sea salt
- 1 stick softened Earth Balance Vegan butter
- 2 tablespoons pure vanilla extract

In a mixing bowl add the first two ingredients mix then add the last three ingredients mix well. Put into the refrigerator for one hour to set up a little you want to use only half of the frosting this makes a lot. Spread on cooled bars. Keep in mind the texture will be different. You can freeze the frosting you have left up to two months.

Original Peppermint Santa's

- 1 cup white morsels
- 2 to 3 drops Natural Peppermint Oil
- 1 drop red food coloring
- Santa candy mold

Add white morsels to a glass microwave dish. Melt for 30 seconds at a time mixing in between until smooth. Add the red food coloring and the peppermint extract mix, fill the Santa mold and tap the mold on the table to even out the melted white morsels. Put into the refrigerator to set about 20 to 25 minutes.

> Note: You can use a Christmas tree mold just use green food coloring and natural wintergreen oil. You can use more then a drop of food coloring this will make your Santa's more red and your Christmas trees more green.

Dairy Free Gluten Free Peppermint Santa's

- 1 cup Pascha Organic white baking chips
- 2 to 3 drops of Natural Peppermint Oil
- 1 drop red food coloring

Add white morsels to a glass microwave dish. Melt for 30 seconds at a time mixing in between until smooth. Add the red food coloring and the peppermint oil mix fill the Santa mold and tap on the table to even out the chocolate. Put into the refrigerator for 20 to 25 minutes.

Original Zucchini Bread

- 2 eggs
- ½ cup canola oil
- 4 tablespoons granulated sugar
- ¼ teaspoons sea salt or table salt
- 1 teaspoon baking powder
- ½ teaspoon baking soda
- ½ cup shredded zucchini
- 1 cup all purpose flour
- ½ cup milk chocolate chips or semi-sweet, optional
- non-stick mini loaf pan, 8 cavity

Preheat the oven to 300 degrees. In a mixing bowl add the first seven ingredients and mix. Add the zucchini mix and all the flour mix well. Add the chocolate chips mix with a spoon. Fill each section with a ¼ cup of batter in each one bake for 30 minutes transfer to a cooling rack.

Tip: If you freeze the zucchini then thaw you will need to squeeze the excess water out of it or your recipe will be watery.

Note: If you freeze 1 cup of zucchini for the bread freeze 2 cups. By the time you squeeze the water out you will end up with 1 cup anyway or a little more.

Gluten Free and Dairy Free Zucchini Bread

- 2 eggs
- ½ cup canola oil
- 4 tablespoons granulated sugar
- ¼ teaspoons sea salt or table salt
- 1 teaspoon Rumfor baking powder
- ½ teaspoon Arm and Hammer baking soda
- ½ cup shredded zucchini
- 1 cup gluten free flour (not the all purpose gluten free flour)
- ½ cup Enjoy life mini chocolate chips or Gefen chocolate chips, optional
- non-stick mini loaf pan, 8 cavity

Preheat the oven to 300 degrees. In a mixing bowl add the first seven ingredients and mix. Add the zucchini all at once mix. Add the flour mix. Add the chocolate chips mix in with a spoon. Fill each section with a ¼ cup of batter in each one bake for 30 minutes transfer to a cooling rack.

Tip: If you freeze the zucchini then thaw you will need to squeeze the excess water out of it or your recipe will be watery.

Note: If you freeze 1 cup of zucchini for the bread freeze 2 cups by the time you squeeze the water out of it you will end up with 1 cup maybe a little more.

Gluten Free & Dairy Free Blueberry Muffins

- 1/2 cup unsweetened original Almond milk
- 1 teaspoon of white vinegar
- In a small bowl mix together Almond milk and vinegar. Let set for 6 minutes.
- 2 eggs
- 1/3 cup canola oil
- 1/2 cup granulated sugar
- 1 teaspoon Baker's Corner baking powder or Stop and Shop baking powder
- ¼ teaspoon Baker's Corner baking soda or Stop and Shop baking soda
- 1 cup gluten free flour, (not the all purpose gluten free flour)
- 1 cup fresh or frozen blueberries
- cupcake liners

Preheat the oven to 350 degrees. In a mixing bowl add milk and vinegar mixture then add the next five ingredients and mix. Add the flour all at once mix well. Add the blueberries mix in with a spoon. Fill the cupcake liners to the top bake for 20 to 25 minutes.

Note: Adding the milk and vinegar mixture makes the muffins tender.

Original Blueberry Muffins

- 1/2 cup whole milk or 1% milk
- 1 teaspoon of white vinegar
- In a small bowl mix together milk and vinegar. Let set for 6 minutes.
- 2 eggs
- 1/3 cup canola oil
- 1/2 cup granulated sugar
- 1 teaspoon baking powder
- ¼ teaspoon baking soda
- 1 cup all purpose flour
- 1 cup fresh or frozen blueberries
- cupcake liners

Preheat the oven to 350 degrees. In a mixing bowl add milk and vinegar mixture then add the next four ingredients and mix. Add the flour all at once mix well. Add the blueberries mix in with a spoon. Fill the cupcake liners to the top bake for 20 to 25 minutes.

Note: Adding the milk and vinegar mixture makes the muffins tender.

Ingredient Information

Sea salt—is all natural and has vitamins, minerals like calcium, zinc, Iron, folate and B12.

Sugars—granulated, light brown, confectionery are gluten free

Alcohol Based Extracts—are gluten free.

Earth Balance Vegan butter sticks—are all natural no dairy of any kind great tasting for baked goods. I have bought this butter at the grocery store your most likely to buy this butter at a health food store.

King Arthur's flavorings and spices—are all gluten free.

King Arthur's Measure for Measure flour—Example: If you use 1 cup measure for measure flour in your gluten free recipes, you would use 1 cup of all purpose flour in your original recipes. The measure to measure flour already has Xanthan gum in it.

King Arthur Pumpkin sugar—Gluten free

Xanthan gum is a common food additive that you find everything and yogurt and of course, gluten-free baked goods. In most cases, it's used as a thickening agent, or as a stabilizer to prevent separation of ingredients (like yogurt).

King Arthur's Cocoa's—are gluten free.

Enjoy Life Semi-sweet Mini Chocolate chips—these are dairy, nut and soy free.

Pascha Organic White baking chips—Are gluten and dairy free, nut free, peanut free, egg free, soy free, wheat free. This product is made with Rice Powder.

Cool Whip—does contain 2% of cream. A lot of whip topping have sodium caseinate which is cows milk that has been converted into sodium caseinate. People who have milk allergies read the labels carefully.

Why people worry about Maltodextrin it may be made from different starches, including corn, potato, rice or wheat. No need to worry the source does not matter because Maltodextrin is a highly processed ingredient that the protein is removed rendering it is gluten free.

Gluten free all purpose flour is used in many recipes but you need to use Xanthan gum with the flour. This will keep your recipe from separating.

Baking powders Baking sodas—take a few tablespoons of white vinegar in a bowl add ½ teaspoon of baking soda or baking powder if it's fresh it will fizz and bubble.

Libby's 100% pumpkin—is gluten free and all natural.

Arm Hammer baking soda—is gluten free and all natural.

Clabber Girl Baking soda—is 100% pure sodium bicarbonate and gluten free.

Rumford Baking Powder—is aluminum free and gluten free.

Smucker's Peanut Butter—gluten free you can buy this at most groceries stores.

Welch's Concord grape jelly—Is gluten free.

Gramma's Molasses—contains no preservatives, artificial flavors or colors is fat free gluten free.

Tofutti Cream Cheese plain—this is glutten free and dairy free.

Natural Peppermint Oil Wintergreen—You can buy this product at amazon.com

Enjoy Life Semi-sweet Chocolate MinChips—You can buy this product at amazon.com

Author Biography

Hi everyone Just wanted to tell you a little bit about myself. I am married to a wonderful guy I have three children and my family is everything to me. I appreciate my mom so much for showing me everything that I know about baking and cooking. I am a person who does not give up easy. I have a dream of having my own show on Food Network someday. I am reaching for the stars and putting together a show to star in to accomplish my dream. Dreams only come true when you go after them. I really enjoy horse back riding, creating my own recipes, walking with my husband, friends, baking, and the word of God. I thank God for all my blessings each day.

www.ingramcontent.com/pod-product-compliance
Lightning Source LLC
Chambersburg PA
CBHW061114070526
44583CB00027B/3294